Praise for

Applied Tarot

An Excessively Practical Guide to Tarot
Card Interpretations

"Life just got simpler and a lot more
fun with this book. Definitely all the
stars!"

~Margaret, Goodreads

"Clever and hilarious!"

~Twitter user

"This book will not tell you how to
divine your destiny, but you'll know
where you put the mailbox key!"

~TJ Deschamps, Author

"Wow, look at you, doing a thing."

~Oscar, Emily's husband

Applied Runes

An Excessively Practical Guide to
Interpreting the Elder Futhark Runes

by Emily Paper

Applied Divination
Redmond

Published by Applied Divination

Front cover image by Emily Paper
Illustrations by Emily Paper
Photographs from Unsplash.com
Book design by Emily Paper

First printing edition 2021

Applied Divination
www.applieddivination.com
info@applieddivination.com

For Maggie,
who descended from the Norsemen but
transcends the gods.

Contents

Introduction

About Runes

Before the Latin alphabet became commonplace, Runes were the letters used in various Germanic and Nordic languages. Runes were also used for decoration, divination, and protection.

There are many Runic alphabets including Celtic, the Dalecarlian, and the Elder Futhark or Norse Runes. This book is focused almost entirely on the Elder Futhark, which is the oldest and most used Runic alphabet in divination, but along the way I will mention other stones and Rune interpretations. The point of Runes is not which ones you use, but in how they can help guide your everyday life.

The English translation and spelling varies in the Elder Futhark, so I have included some different spellings for each within these pages.

How to use this book

This book is a reference, not a novel. You do not need to read it front to back, nor should you. This book is for answering basic questions with Runes, and assumes you have a bag of Runes on hand. (If you do not currently have Runes, please skip to page 4 and create your own set. It's easy!)

Steps:
1. Ask your question.
2. Mix up the Runes and pull one out.

3. Skip to the page for the Rune pulled, and hopefully you will get some functional insight.

If you *do not* get any functional insight, you can attempt a wordier answer by using the two-Rune combinations on each page, or the three-Rune sentence maker on Page 7.

Finally, understand that if the individual interpretations do not help, or the combinations calculator spews randomness, your question might not have a simple answer and you might need a legit fortune teller to help you figure things out. Good luck with that!

A quick note on movie recommendations: A good movie falls into several themes, so take my suggestions lightly. These are all movies that are fairly-well known, that I have personally seen, and that fit the category.
If you have movie or book recommendations, contact me through www.emilypaper.com

Bindrunes

Bindrunes are exactly as they sound - it is the binding of two or more Runes into one character. While the Norse tribes did not often write this way, when Vikings brought the Runes to Iceland, the Icelandic people combined them, and their Runic alphabet possesses bindrunes to this day.
You can create your own Bindrunes by pulling two Runes and drawing an image of how they might fit together. I have

included two-Rune combinations in all the individual descriptors in this book.

Keep in mind not all Runes were combined this way historically, so my interpretations are personal opinions at best. If you have suggested bindrune combination meanings, let me know!

Reversals

An upside-down Rune can be just as important as a Rune that is right side up. However, not all Runes have reversals, and those that do may have meanings that vary depending on the question asked. In that regard, I only touch upon reversals lightly for each Rune. You can rest assured that even a positive, irreversible Rune has its negative values, so it should be fairly easy to figure out what the worst-case scenario of a Rune might be.

Here are a few relatively simple ways to incorporate reversals into your readings:

1. Interpret the Runes as the opposite of an upright meaning. For example, the opposite of strength (Uruz or Thurisaz, for example) is weakness.

2. Interpret the Runes as being more specific or local to you. For example, instead of a vacation to Scotland to see the beautiful Yew trees (Ihwaz), go to your local nursery and admire a Yew there.

3. Interpret the Rune with a more negative meaning (or positive if the Rune upright is traditionally negative.) For example, the

reverse of chance and fortune (Perthro) is refusing to take a risk or having bad luck.

What if I Do Not Have Runes?

The images in this book are my own creation. Some are Runes I created in my free time, some are store-bought Runes I had lying around my house, and others were ones I photoshopped using pics from Unsplash.com. Runes featured in this book are not and will never be for sale, because manufacturing Runes is absurd when my readers can easily make Runes themselves or buy them very cheaply! It takes no time at all to draw on some stones.

There are only 24 Runes to create, and the symbols are comprised of simple lines. You could be like the Norse tribes and carve rocks, wood, or bone with a knife. It is believed that the first Runes were carved into the wood of the Yew or Birch trees, as these were plentiful and sturdy in the cold Norse climate. If carving is not your thing, I recommend a simple sharpie and some garden stones. Anything that lasts is good, as your Runes may get a lot of wear and tear.

The simplest option is to draw the Runic alphabet on index cards, and shuffle them like tarot cards.

Runes are also available inexpensively from online shops such as Etsy or Amazon. They are sold in a variety of materials including bones, wood, tiles, and crystals.

While the Germanic and Norse tribes did not use crystals for special divination purposes, here are some historically medicinal crystals that are readily available as Runes in online shopping sites, and their associated medicinal value:

Tiger's Eye
Spending, joy

Carnelian
Physical energy, confidence, luck

Obsidian
Protection

Citrine or Amber
Hearing, pain, and sleep management

Smoky Quartz
Safe travel, meeting new people, focus

Jade
Intelligence, contentment

Rose Quartz
Love, pregnancy, and nourishment

Amethyst
Calmness, courage

Labradorite
Happiness, enlightenment

Aquamarine
Safety, vision

Drawing or Carving the Runes

Here are the shapes you will need to carve or draw. Names and their associated meanings will come later, as we discuss the 3 sets, or aettir.

ᚠ	Fehu	ᚺ	Hagalaz	↑	Tiwaz
ᚢ	Uruz	ᚾ	Nauthiz	ᛒ	Berkano
ᚦ	Thurisaz	ᛁ	Isa	ᛗ	Ehwaz
ᚨ	Ansuz	ᛃ	Jera	ᛗ	Mannaz
ᚱ	Raido	ᛇ	Ihwaz	ᛚ	Laguz
ᚲ	Kaunaz	ᛈ	Perthro	ᛜ	Inguz
ᚷ	Gebo	ᛉ	Algiz	ᛟ	Othala
ᚹ	Wunjo	ᛋ	Sowelo	ᛞ	Dagaz

Alternate Spelling for the Runes

Throughout the book I may use alternate spellings for the Runes, either for size or just to introduce you to the many wonderful surprises from this ancient Anglo-Saxon language. Other informational books about Runes may use different orthography as the primary spelling.

A few of the many alternate Rune spellings:

Fehu: Feoh, Fe
Uruz: Ur
Thurisaz: Thorn, Thurs
Ansuz: As
Raido: Raidho, Rad
Kaunaz: Kenaz, Ken
Gebo: Gifu, Gyfu
Wunjo: Wynn
Hagalaz: Hagal, Haegl
Nauthiz: Nyd, Naudiz
Isa: Isar, Is
Jera: Jeran, Jeraz, Ger

Ihwaz: Eiwaz, Eoh
Perthro: Peorth
Algiz: Elhaz
Sowelo: Sigel, Sol
Tiwaz: Teiwaz, Tyr
Berkano: Beorc, Beroc
Ehwaz: Eoh, Eh, Ehwar
Mannaz: Mann, Madhr
Laguz: Lagu, Logr
Inguz: Ing, Ingwar
Othala: Odal
Dagaz: Daeg, Dagar

Sentence Combinations

I have created this table of words using some of the most rudimentary interpretations from each Rune.

In Runes, each stone represents a variety of meanings based on different contexts, so this combinations list is not at all inclusive, nor does it have any meaning besides being something fun to try on a dull day.

You can use the following words in any combination and in any structure of phrase. When I ask a question, I typically pick three Runes and as each Rune is drawn, I order them:

Verb > Adjective > Noun

Some prepositions you could add between the Runes are: about, with, of, at, for, regarding, by, etc.

Please keep in mind that the Germanic and Norse people did not create sentences with Runes this way. They took all the Rune meanings into account and thought seriously about the messages and warnings they were receiving from the Gods.
This is a fun sentence construct game I like to play, because I have a simple mind and this is not a mystical divination book, these are straightforward and practical interpretations for your set of Runes.

Rune	Sound	Verb	Adjective	Noun
Fehu	ᚠ	f	Spend	Successful	Riches
Uruz	ᚢ	oo	Empower	Strong	Courage
Thurisaz	ᚦ	th	Defend	Protective	Chaos
Ansuz	ᚨ	ah	Speak	Inspiring	Reason
Raido	ᚱ	r	Initiate	Active	Journey
Kaunaz	ᚲ	k	Clarify	Intelligent	Study
Gebo	ᚷ	g	Exchange	Generous	Gifts
Wunjo	ᚹ	v, w	Believe	Joyful	Hope
Hagalaz	ᚺ	h	Surrender	Tragic	Crisis
Nauthiz	ᚾ	n	Resist	Conflicting	Necessity
Isa	ᛁ	ee	Focus	Stagnant	Identity
Jera	ᛃ	y	Harvest	Patient	Year
Ihwaz	ᛇ	ai	Endure	Persevering	Longevity
Pertho	ᛈ	p	Gamble	Mysterious	Chance
Algiz	ᛉ	z	Protect	Divine	Awakening
Sowelo	ᛋ	ss	Celebrate	Successful	Victory
Tyr	ᛏ	t	Sacrifice	Rational	Justice
Berkano	ᛒ	b	Nourish	Fertile	Birth
Ehwaz	ᛗ	eh	Trust	Cooperative	Team
Mannaz	ᛗ	m	Learn	Intelligent	Mind
Laguz	ᛚ	l	Imagine	Unconscious	Dreams
Inguz	ᛜ	ng	Create	Ambitious	Evolution
Othala	ᛟ	oh	Inherit	Ancestral	Legacy
Dagaz	ᛞ	d	Awaken	Enlightened	Dawn

I'm feeling lazy and unambitious today, so I asked the Runes "How can I motivate myself?" I drew:

C   ↑   M

Pertho >   **Tyr** >   **Mannaz**

Using the combinations calculator in Verb/adjective/noun form, I get "Gamble (with) rational mind."

I've interpreted that to mean "allow yourself to be irrational," which allows me to take some pressure off myself.

Pairs are included in the Rune pages. They might expand on these super quick references, or they will show different ways the Runes can be combined for your situation.

Now, go forth and...

Inguz   Kaunaz   Thurisaz

Verb: Adjective: Noun:
Create   **Intelligent**   **Chaos**

Or merely have some fun with it all**!**

The Three Aettir

What are the Aettir?

The Elder Futhark Runes are separated into three aettir (singular: aett.) Aett is a Norse word with no definitive translation, but it is akin to *family* or *generation*.

The aettir of Runes represent three stages. What those stages are is up to you, but examples could be the stages of education (student, master, elder), ability (novice, trainee, expert), gender (female, male, non-binary) or whatever strikes you in the moment. The Vikings may have divided them into nurturer, warrior, and priest. If you are consulting the Runes about *your* life, you might divide them into childhood, adolescence, and adulthood.

While each aett has its own feel or theme, no aett is better nor worse than the others. They all share both positive and negative Runes, as well as Runes with common themes. For example, each aett has one or two stones representing wealth, emotion, element, or method of travel.

Just like each stage of one's life possesses similar themes, so does each aett of the Runes.

Freya's Aett

Freya is the Norse god of fertility, love, and beauty. The Runes attributed to Freya are about beginnings, femininity, and joyfulness.

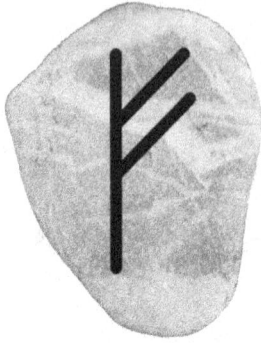

Fehu
"f"

**Wealth
Cattle**

Fehu is wealth. But rather than being
static savings, such as property or a
retirement account, Fehu is money that
moves. Much like farmer's cattle, the money
comes in, moves around, grows, and goes out
again. Fehu is your constantly liquid
earnings, social status, and power.

One way to memorize this Rune meaning
is to imagine it's a stick-figure person,
holding up two arms to receive wealth. It
also looks like a wonky "F," which is the
letter Fehu represents.

The reverse of Fehu is greed, poverty,
or failure

Fehu as:
An action?
- Donate to a charity
- Accept a gift being given to you

A place in your house?
- The kitchen
- Your money or wallet

A place in your city?
- The bank
- A nonprofit
- An investment firm

A place in the world?
- Singapore
- Wall Street
- The Caymans
- Switzerland

Something to eat?
- A healthy, well-balanced meal
- Steak
- Snacks on the go, such as energy bars

A color? Red, purple
A gemstone? Agate

A movie theme? Luck, wealth, spending
- Wall Street
- It Could Happen to You
- Catch Me if You Can
- Robin Hood

A new career?
- Philanthropist
- Broker or loan officer
- Artist or actor
- Cab driver

Questions answered by Fehu:

Who? A lucky and generous person
What? The circulation of money
Where? Where the money flows
When? The Beginning of July; Payday
Why? What you give to the world, you receive back in kind
Yes or No? Yes **Reversed?** No

What should I clean?
- The closet
- The kitchen
- Clear out some unpaid bills
- Send out your invoices for the month

Where are my missing keys?
- In your purse or briefcase
- You left them in the car

Combos - Fehu says *spend your money* on

Uruz – fitness
Thurisaz - defense
Ansuz – a new phone
Raido - travel
Kaunaz – school supplies
Gebo – gifts for others
Wunjo - friends
Hagal - transformation
Nauthiz – your needs
Isa - rest
Jera - plants
Ihwaz - transformation

Pertho - games
Algiz - protection
Sowelo - goals
Tiwaz – just causes
Berkano - healing
Ehwaz – your partner
Mannaz - humankind
Laguz – clean water
Inguz - seeds
Odal- your household
Dagaz – another day

Uruz

"oo"

Strength
Speed
Aurochs

Uruz looks like an upside-down U and sounds like *oo*, so it's fairly easy to learn.

Represented by the Auroch (an extinct species of wild cattle,) Uruz is your vitality, physical health, independence and life force.

Where Fehu represented your domesticated cattle (wealth), Uruz reminds us that animals are innately wild, and it's that ferocity and passion that Uruz stands for. When Uruz is pulled, it's time to use your inner warrior to endure a situation or manifest success.

The reverse of Uruz is rage and insensitivity.

Uruz as:
An action?
- Go for a run
- Eat a huge meal
- Learn something new

A place in your house?
- The fitness area or gym equipment
- The kitchen
- The shower

A place in your city?
- The gym
- The park
- Your favorite restaurant

A place in the world?
- Northern Europe
- Alaska
- Poland
- Strongman, Olympics, or another competition

Something to eat?
- A protein bar
- Grasses and grains
- An animal you hunted and cooked yourself

A color? Green, brown
A gemstone? Garnet

A movie theme? Strength, survival
- Gladiator
- The Hunger Games
- The Revenant

A new career?
- Veterinary or human medicine
- Human Resources
- Manual Labor

Questions answered by Uruz:

Who? Your personal trainer; a zoologist
What? Your inner reserves; your most basic instincts; survival
Where? The gym
When? Mid-late July; During sunny weather; when the cows come home
Why? "Freedom, in any case, is only possible by constantly struggling for it." ~Albert Einstein
Yes or No? Yes, if you are strong enough
Reversed? No

Something interesting: The Uruz Project
https://en.wikipedia.org/wiki/Uruz_Project

What should I clean?
- Exercise equipment
- Bathe the dog or empty the litterbox

Where are my missing keys?
- On the treadmill or wherever you work out
- Near your pet

Combos: Uruz says *manifest or fight for*

Fehu - spending money
Thurisaz - safety gear
Ansuz - freedom of speech
Raido - righteousness
Kaunaz - education
Gebo - gift giving
Wunjo - happiness
Hagal - transformation
Nauthiz - innovation
Isa - self-preservation
Jera - life changes
Ihwaz - longevity

Pertho - your destiny
Algiz - connection
Sowelo - mastery
Tiwaz - justice
Berkano - new growth
Ehwaz - the team
Mann - social programs
Laguz - clean water
Ing - self empowerment
Othala - your legacy
Dagaz - your ideal self

Thurisaz
"th"

Chaos
Transformation
Thorn

Thurisaz is the God Thor's Rune. When we
think about Thor, even the character from
the Marvel Cinematic Universe, we think of
weapons, self-empowerment, and a person who
defends their realm. That's the meaning of
Thurisaz.

The easiest way to recognize Thurisaz
is to see the image as a thorn sticking out
of a branch. Imagine it protecting you from
something on the other side.

The reverse of Thurisaz is disease or
senseless violence.

Thurisaz as:
An action?
- Stand up for what you believe in
- Join a protest or challenge yourself in something new

A place in your house?
- The front porch
- The garden
- The toolbox or tool shed

A place in your city?
- A martial arts school
- A challenging workplace

A place in the world?
- Norway
- Vietnam
- Greece and Mesopotamia

Something to eat?
- Citrus and apples
- Blackberries
- Try an intermittent fasting diet (Aasgardian gods often fast for long periods of time)

A color? Crimson, blue
A gemstone? Sapphire

A movie theme? Defense, weapons, protection
- Thor
- Independence Day
- Wonder Woman

A new career?
- Nonfiction writer or copyeditor
- Bodyguard or Security
- Construction or farm work

Questions answered by Thurisaz:

Who? The most defensive person
What? A challenge
Where? A basecamp; one's house
When? The beginning of August; During a difficult ("thorny") time period
Why? Stiff competition is good for you
Yes or No? Yes **Reversed?** No

What should I clean?
- The front hall
- The window
- The knife drawer or weapons storage

Where are my missing keys?
- In a place you need to secure, such as a vault or fine china cabinet
- Inside the front door

Combos: Thurisaz says *protect your*

Fehu - wallet
Uruz - independence
Ansuz - opinion
Raido - vehicle
Kaunaz - creative flow
Gebo - material goods
Wunjo - community
Hagalaz - shelter
Nauthiz - efforts
Isa - ego
Jera - growing seeds
Ihwaz - mysteries

Pertho - emotions
Algiz - higher self
Sowelo - positivity
Tiwaz - principles
Berkano - sanctuary
Ehwaz - emotions
Mannaz - mind
Laguz - memories
Inguz - inner child
Othala - legacy
Dagaz - ideal self

Ansuz

"ah"

Speech
Expression
God

Ansuz is the divine voice of Odin, who breathed wisdom into humans and inspired our unique cognitive processes and communication ability.

In a more practical use, the Rune is associated with intellect, mental activity, and speech.

Ansuz looks like another wonky letter F, but I like to imagine it as a stick figure person speaking and gesturing to a crowd below them, kind of like Socrates on a staircase.

This is silly, but imagine Socrates saying "..and I says to 'im, I says…" *and I says,* muffled, could be *Ansuz*.

The reverse of Ansuz is bad advice or misunderstanding.

Ansuz as:
An action?
- Learn something new
- Network and make new connections
- Trust your intuition

A place in your house?
- The bookshelf
- An area where things are discussed

A place in your city?
- An institution of higher learning
- A library

A place in the world?
- Athens, Greece
- Japan
- Finland
- India
- Washington DC
- London, England

Something to eat?
- Cashews
- Whole grain deli sandwich
- Bananas
- Salmon

A color? Deep blue and black
A gemstone? Emerald

A movie theme? A studious mind, Odin
- Good Will Hunting
- Thor
- Bill & Ted's Excellent Adventure

A new career?
- Communications and Informatics
- Politics
- Professor or orator

Questions answered by Ansuz:

Who? A speaker
What? A lesson
Where? College or university
When? August; The first day of school; When the speech happens
Why? News is coming
Yes or No? Yes, but listen to your inner voice **Reversed?** Maybe, but be careful of bad advice

What should I clean?
- Bookshelf or educational area
- The office desk

Where are my missing keys?
- Under a book
- Where you last had a conversation

Combos: Ansuz says *talk to people about*

Fehu - money
Uruz – physical health
Thurisaz – life changes
Raido - vacations
Kaunaz - inspiration
Gebo - presents
Wunjo – the weather
Hagal - transformation
Nauthiz - needs
Isa – self-control
Jera – gardening
Ihwaz – transformation

Pertho - mysteries
Algiz - spirituality
Sowelo– hopes & dreams
Tiwaz - justice
Berkano - parenting
Ehwaz - teamwork
Mann – social order
Laguz - dreams
Inguz – genesis
Othala-estate planning
Dagaz – spiritual awakening

Raido

"r"

**Journey
Travel
Wheel**

Raido is easy. Raido looks like an R,
sounds like an R, and basically means
"ride," which starts with an R.

It represents our personal life
journey as well as the small trips and
different paths our daily actions might
take us on. When we are suffering, Raido
indicates that there might be a different
path right in front of us. Take it!

The reverse of Raido is immobility,
restlessness, or a control freak.

Raido as:
An action?
- Go for a drive
- Choose a new direction
- Buy a new car

A place in your house?
- The main entrance
- Your garage

A place in your city?
- The bus terminal
- The car dealership
- The highway out of town

A place in the world?
- France
- Heathrow Airport
- The Indianapolis Motor Speedway
- A theme park

Something to eat?
- Nutrition bar
- A sandwich
- A milk shake
- Fast food

A color? Red
A gemstone? Chalcedony

A movie theme? Travel, decisions, races
- Cars
- Interstellar
- Run Lola Run
- Cool Runnings

A new career?
- Race car driver!
- Transport driver, long haul trucker, or dispatcher
- Networking
- Quality control

Questions answered by Raido:

Who? The person in the driver's seat
What? Street smarts
Where? The tracks; the garage
When? The beginning of September; back to school time
Why? "Travel is the only thing you buy that makes you richer." ~Anonymous
Yes or No? Yes, if you plan **Reversed?** No

What should I clean?
- The car

Where are my missing keys?
- The car

Combos: Raido says *travel is required for*

Fehu – more money
Uruz – independence
Thurisaz – willpower
Ansuz - conversation
Kaunaz - education
Gebo – trade/exchange
Wunjo - community
Hagal – radical change
Nauthiz - innovation
Isa – rest
Jera – harvesting change
Ihwaz - perseverance

Pertho – destiny
Algiz-divine messages
Sowelo - guidance
Tiwaz - justice
Berkano – a fresh start
Ehwaz - partnership
Mann - intelligence
Laguz - inspiration
Inguz - self growth
Othala - inheritance
Dagaz - awakening

Kaunaz

"K"

Knowledge
Wood
Torchlight

Kaunaz, Ken, or Kenaz looks like its first
letter K, but without the vertical line.

It literally means "torch," but can be
thought of as a lightbulb above one's head
– it is indicative of the acquisition of
knowledge, an improvement in skill, or a
flash of clarity.

Remember that we learn more from our
mistakes than we do our successes, so there
is sometimes an ominous warning when Kaunaz
comes up.

The reverse of Kaunaz is ignorance or
lack of creativity.

Kaunaz as:
An action?
- Take a class
- Practice a skill
- Start a project

A place in your house?
- The office
- The kitchen
- A crafts area
- The workshop

A place in your city?
- A school
- An art gallery
- A library
- A lighting store

A place in the world?
- Lofoten Islands
- New Zealand
- Northern Canada
- Tasmania

Something to eat?
- Blueberries
- Vitamin D
- Chocolate
- Superfoods

A color? Green, light red
A gemstone? Bloodstone

A movie theme? Art, skill, knowledge
- Gattaca
- A Beautiful Mind
- Slumdog Millionaire

A new career?
- Electrician
- Career coach
- Artist or skilled craftsman
- Obstetrics and Gynecology

Questions answered by Kaunaz:

Who? Someone who knows a remarkable amount for her or his age or position; someone with a surprising talent
What? A new idea
Where? An interesting shop you have never visited
When? The end of September; the equinox
Why? "A woman with knowledge is something that frightens the status quo quite a lot."
~ Helen Mirren
Yes or No? Yes, but education is required
Reversed? No, you do not know enough

What should I clean?
- Your crafts space
- Your home office

Where are my missing keys?
- Near a lamp
- On your desk

Combos: Kaunaz says *learn about*

Fehu - finances
Uruz - fitness
Thurisaz - tools
Ansuz - religion
Raido - transportation
Gebo - cultural gifts
Wunjo - the weather
Hagal - climate change
Nauthiz - consequences
Isa - self-control
Jera - gardening
Ihwaz - immortality

Pertho - prophecies
Algiz - the Valkyries
Sowelo - goalsetting
Tyr - laws, justice
Berkano - motherhood
Ehwaz - your partner
Mannaz - humanity
Laguz - the ocean
Ing - self development
Othala-estate planning
Dagaz - spiritual awakening

Gebo

"G"

**Exchange
Union
Gift**

Gebo is a tough one to remember, because it looks like a giant X, which naturally turns us off from it. But if we think of it in terms of an eXchange, we can better visualize it as a reciprocation.

You could also imagine the X in X-mas to remember how X marks gift-giving.

In Viking times, Gebo also suggested a trade between powers – a way to dissolve barriers by presenting presents to one another.

Gebo has no reverse, as exchange happens regardless of its goodness or badness.

Gebo as:
An action?
- Donate to a charity
- Give someone a gift
- Make a trade

Place in your house?
- The kitchen
- A pile of things to be donated

Place in your city?
- A gift shop
- A nonprofit
- An investment firm

Place in the world?
- Japan
- Iceland
- China
- Romania

Something to eat?
- Lasagna or a pasta casserole
- Wine
- A Thanksgiving meal

A color? Dark blue
A gemstone? Opal

A movie theme? generosity, giving
- The Grinch
- Pay it Forward
- The Nightmare Before Christmas
- Robin Hood

A new career?
- Philanthropist
- Broker or loan officer
- Pastor or wedding officiant

33

Questions answered by Gebo:

Who? A generous person
What? A gift
Where? In someone else's possession
When? The Beginning of October; At the next gift-giving event
Why? What you give to the world, you receive back in kind;

> Ever Mind the Rule of Three, Three Times Your Acts Return to Thee.
> This Lesson Well Thou Must Learn, Thou Only Gets What Thee Dost Earn[14]

Yes or No? Maybe, you give what you get

What should I clean?
- Take out the garbage or recycling
- The wrapping paper closet

Where are my missing keys?
- You handed them to someone

Combos: Gebo says *give the gift of*

Fehu - money	**Pertho** - mystery
Uruz – fitness equipment	**Algiz** - protection
Thurisaz - roses	**Sowelo** - smiles, sun
Ansuz – a phone call	**Tiwaz** - honesty
Raido – a trip	**Berkano** - renewal
Kaunaz – a flashlight	**Ehwaz** – a pet
Wunjo - joy	**Mann** – good memories
Hagalaz – change	**Laguz** - water
Nauthiz - innovation	**Inguz** - seeds
Isa - rest	**Othala** – inheritance
Jera – a plant	**Dagaz** – another day
Ihwaz - longevity	

---

[14] The "rule of three," a pagan karmic philosophy that applies to both good and bad behavior: What you give out, you receive back in triplicate, so give good things!

Wunjo

"V" or "W"

Wind
Hope
Joy

Wunjo is positive, hopeful joy. Its Norse meaning is wind, so we can imagine that when things are difficult, change will come on the next gust of wind.

To remember this Rune's meaning, imagine it looks like the letter "p" and positivity is blowing in. The actual sound it makes is "w", for wind.

This is the Rune of will and motivation. Like the butterfly effect, the wind blows harder when we make a move.

The reverse of Wunjo is caution, hopelessness, or betrayal.

Wunjo as:
An action?
- Throw a party
- Water Plants
- Visualize the future you want

A place in your house?
- The air conditioner
- The living room
- The phone

A place in your city?
- Community center
- A restaurant
- A gathering place
- A park

A place in the world?
- Denmark
- Nepal
- New Zealand

Something to eat?
- Comfort food
- A buffet
- Dinner with friends

A color? Orange, brown, yellow
A gemstone? Diamond

A movie theme? Joy, motivation, wind
- Up!
- La La Land
- The Boy Who Harnessed the Wind

A new career?
- Entertainer or event organizer
- Public servant
- Meteorologist

Questions answered by Wunjo:

Who? The happiest person; the motivated one
What? The weather forecast
Where? High up
When? The middle of October; on a windy day
Why? "When the winds of change blow, some people build walls and others build windmills." ~Chinese Proverb
Yes or No? Yes! **Reversed?** Maybe, be cautious

What should I clean?
- The oven vent
- The dishes
- Clear the garden of loose items that could blow away in a storm

Where are my missing keys?
- Near a vent
- A party room

Combos: Wunjo says *motivate yourself to*

Fehu – make money
Uruz – work out
Thurisaz – protest
Ansuz – make a speech
Raido – run an errand
Kaunaz - study
Gebo - unionize
Hagalaz - transform
Nauthiz – do chores
Isa – take a break
Jera – plant seeds
Ihwaz – transform

Pertho – take a chance
Algiz – listen
Sowelo – take action
Tiwaz – be honest
Berkano - grow
Ehwaz – work together
Mannaz – make plans
Lagz– trust intuition
Ing– develop oneself
Othala–create a legacy
Dagaz - awaken

Hagal's Aett

Hagal means hail, and the Runes in Hagal's aett are about weather, achievement, and disruptive forces.

Hagalaz

"H"

Crisis
Risks
Hail

Hagalaz literally translates to *hail*. In more esoteric divinations, it is about discord and destruction.

We can imagine hail pelting us - it stings and is relentless, but it soon melts and nourishes the Earth. Transformation occurs after this time of painful crisis.

Picture the Rune as an H standing for Hagalaz, but the middle line is wonky and chaotic, which represents its meaning.

Hagal has no reverse, as the opposite of chaos is just more chaos.

Hagalaz as:
An action?
- Quit a job
- Move houses
- End a relationship

A place in your house?
- The freezer
- The medicine cabinet
- The mailbox

A place in your city?
- A weather station
- An institution with chaotic meaning for you
- A shelter

A place in the world?
- Earth's fault lines
- Kauai, Hawaii
- Meghalaya, India
- A place of great upheaval

Something to eat?
- Random snacks
- An apple
- Peppers
- Iced coffee
- Vegan food if you are an omnivore (or vice versa)

A color? Light blue, white
A gemstone? Onyx

A movie theme? Chaos, bad weather
- Titanic
- Twister
- Jurassic Park
- Sharknado

A new career?
- Environmental Scientist
- Freelancer
- Ski instructor

Questions answered by Hagalaz:

Who? Someone who has recently gone through a difficult time
What? Emergency prep; imminent disaster
Where? A place where disaster has struck
When? October-November; Samhain, or the first day of winter; rapidly
Why? "Maybe you needed to get whacked hard by life before you understood what you wanted out of it." ~*Jodi Picoult*
Yes or No? No.

What should I clean?
- The worst mess

Where are my missing keys?
- You dropped them somewhere terrible, like down a storm drain or the toilet

Combos: Hagalaz says *change your mind about*

Fehu - money
Uruz - your passions
Thurisaz - defenses
Ansuz - intelligence
Raido - travel
Kaunaz - classes
Gebo - a gift
Wunjo - the weather
Nauthiz - hard work
Isa - waiting
Jera - the seasons
Ihwaz - dissatisfaction
Pertho - taking chances
Algiz - divine messages
Sowelo - your goals
Tyr - your principles
Berkano - dependence
Ehwaz - the team
Mannaz - the masses
Laguz - the occult
Inguz - expectations
Othala - your legacy
Dagaz - hopelessness

Bindrune bonus: The symbol for Bluetooth is a combination of the younger Futhark symbol for Hagal "h", and Berkano "b." It is the initials of Danish king Harald I, who was nicknamed Harold Bluetooth.

Nauthiz
"N"

Stress
Necessity
"Not This"
Need

Nauthiz literally translates to "need fire." It comes when we're toiling away at difficult tasks, when we're in conflict with our current situation, or when there is an urgency to be doing anything else or *be* anywhere else.

While a more mundane interpretation might be basic chores, it is also about the self-reliance and effort needed to push through and get to the other side.

Nauthiz looks like two sticks rubbing together, as if we are desperately trying to create the *fire* that we *need* to get through whatever we're suffering.

The easiest way to remember the name and meaning is Naut-thiz "oh no, *NOT THIS*!"

The reverse of Nauthiz or Nyd is an inability to see that change is needed.

Nauthiz as:
An action?
- Do the mundane chores
- Pick the lesser of two evils
- Learn from your mistakes

A place in your house?
- The laundry room
- The eaves or gutters
- Anywhere you don't want to be

A place in your city?
- The police station
- Work, school, or wherever you don't want to be

A place in the world?
- Poison gardens, England
- La Rinconada, Peru
- A family reunion

Something to eat?
- Cilantro
- Candy corn
- Durian
- Pineapple pizza

A color? Black, grey
A gemstone? Lapis Lazuli

A movie theme? Boredom, chores, fire
- The Truman Show
- The Big Lebowski
- Backdraft
- The Handmaid's Tale

A new career?
- Administrative work
- Script supervisor
- Welder

Questions answered by Nauthiz:

Who? An accountant; a bored person
What? A difficult chore
Where? A fire pit; right in front of you
When? Mid-late November; in the thick of it
Why? "A rat in a maze is free to go anywhere, as long as it stays inside the maze." ~Margaret Atwood, A Handmaid's Tale
Yes or No? Maybe - it is up to you

What should I clean?

- The bathroom
- The dishwasher drain

Where are my missing keys?

- The last place you were unhappy
- Under the sink

Combos: **Nauthiz says *recognize the lesson in***

Fehu - paying bills
Uruz - persistence
Thurisaz - chaos
Ansuz - discussion
Raidho - common sense
Kaunaz - tradition
Gebo - giving
Wunjo - wishful thinking
Hagalaz - catastrophe
Isa - delays
Jera - changing times
Ihwaz - boredom

Pertho - taking risks
Algiz - listening
Sowelo - bad advice
Tiwaz - sacrifice
Berkano - healing
Ehwaz - trust
Mannaz - planning
Laguz - dreaming
Inguz - resting
Othala- disinheritance
Dagaz - cataclysmic change

Isa
"ee"

**Static
Ice**

We can imagine what the cold Norse winters
were like, with the earth covered in frost
and the landscape barely traversable for
months on end. This is what Isa represents
– a static ice, harsh but beautiful, that
hides the Earth before its glorious spring
transformation.

Isa encourages us to wait, put a stop
to our ego, and don't try anything
spontaneous. Spring always follows winter,
do not rush it.

Isa has no reverse, as ice is not just
some challenge that must be overcome, it is
the very nature of a polar environment.

Isa as:
An action?
- Wait it out
- Take a nap
- Meditate

A place in your house?
- The freezer
- The coldest room

A place in your city?
- An ice bar
- A church
- A break room
- An abandoned building
- Undeveloped land

A place in the world?
- The poles
- Russia
- An Ice World theme park

Something to eat?
- Ice Cream
- Celery
- Cold water

A color? Black, white, metallic
A gemstone? Tiger's Eye

A movie theme? Ice, delays
- The Empire Strikes Back
- Frozen
- Inception
- Office Space
- Breakfast Club

A new career?
- Sales
- Construction worker
- Postal service worker

Questions answered by Isa:

Who? Someone between jobs; the coldest
person
What? A delay
Where? A rest stop
When? The beginning of December; after a
long wait
Why? "Winter passes and one remembers one's
perseverance" ~ Yoko Ono
Yes or No? Not now

What should I clean?
- The fridge
- The bedsheets

Where are my missing keys?
- The last place you were lying down

**Combos: Isa says *Control yourself when it
comes to***

Fehu - spending
Uruz - exercise
Thurisaz - life changes
Ansuz - what you say
Raido - travel plans
Kaunaz - education
Gebo - gift giving
Wunjo - sudden moves
Hagal - taking risks
Nauthiz - escape attempts
Jera - seeds you plant
Ihwaz - dissatisfaction

Pertho - gambling
Algiz - facing danger
Sowelo - goalsetting
Tiwaz - decisions
Berkano - secrets
Ehwaz - emotions
Mann - self-delusion
Laguz - manipulation
Inguz - immaturity
Othala - the estate
Dagaz - hopelessness

Jera

"Y"

Harvest
Cycle
Year

Like Isa reminds us that nature slows when
it needs to, Jera reminds us that a
bountiful harvest is inevitable, too.

Jera represents those moments between
seasons, and how they blend to create
natural cycles of abundance and loss,
marriage and divorce, planting and
harvesting, or what have you.

Imagine Jera as two sides of a square
that never closes. Just as we naturally
oppose ourselves and each other when things
change, Jera is a cycle that is never
complete.

Jera has no reverse, as the cycles of
time continue regardless of circumstances.

Jera as:
An action?
- Garden
- Have a baby
- Take your chances

A place in your house?
- The plants
- The entryway

A place in your city?
- A florist
- The supermarket
- A psychotherapist's office

A place in the world?
- Places with intense seasonality, such as the Northeastern US
- The Yangtze river valley
- Any arable, highly fertile land

Something to eat?
- Golden fruits
- Tomatoes
- Rice
- Hemp

A color? Light blue or green
A gemstone? Carnelian

A movie theme? Gardening, cycles of life
- The Lion King
- The Secret Garden
- Wall-E
- The Martian

A new career?
- Get in at the very beginning, such as venture capitalism or a startup
- Farmer
- Climatologist
- Pop-up shops and food trucks

Questions answered by Jera:

Who? The gardener
What? A seed
Where? Near the plants
When? The end of December or end of the year; when the seasons change; the harvest
Why? "Always do your best. What you plant now, you will harvest later." ~Og Mandino
Yes or No? Maybe. As this Rune cannot be reversed, only that which has been sown shall be reaped.

What should I clean?
- Weed the garden
- Make room for a new baby or pet

Where are my missing keys?
- Near the plants

Jera says plant seeds now to later harvest

Fehu - money
Uruz - power
Thurisaz - safety
Ansuz - wisdom
Raido - a vacation
Kaunaz - education
Gebo - gifts
Wunjo - joy
Hagal - radical change
Nauthiz - needs
Isa - identity
Ihwaz - transformation

Pertho - the unknown
Algiz - protection
Sowelo - success
Tiwaz - fair justice
Berkano - new growth
Ehwaz - trust
Mannaz - memories
Laguz - intuition
Inguz - personal time
Othala - prosperity
Dagaz - enlightenment

Bindrune bonus: the preceding Rune Isa and the next Rune Ihwaz, combine to form a variant of Jera. It is often called the Lantern Rune due to it's lantern-like appearance. It also means cycles.

Ihwaz
"ai"

Quest
Perseverance
Yew tree

The Yew tree is one of the world's oldest
evergreens. It lives for thousands of years
and possesses poisonous needles that affect
the central nervous system.

In that regard, we can picture the
Rune as a stick representing the Yew, with
poisonous needles on each tip. As the Rune
cannot be reversed, it is about unchanging
perseverance, what happens when we die, and
immortality.

Ihwaz can not be reversed, as the
mysteries surrounding death and eternity
are not for us to solve.

Ihwaz as:
An action?
- Plant seeds
- Buy a plant

A place in your house?
- A tree
- The garden
- The foundation

A place in your city?
- A historical building
- A park with a forest

A place in the world?
- Egypt
- Athens
- Mesopotamia
- Fortinghall, Scotland[15]
- Bermiego, Spain[15]

Something to eat?
- Pot roast
- Soufflé
- Homemade bread

A color? Dark blue, green
A gemstone? Topaz

A movie theme? Perseverance, immortality
- Forrest Gump
- The Shawshank Redemption
- The Age of Adeline

A new career?
- Treecutter, firefighter, forest ranger
- Go back to school to master a subject
- Nonprofit work

---

[15] Two of the oldest Yew trees in the world can be found in these villages

Questions answered by Ihwaz:
Who? The person who works with trees
What? A transformational period
Where? Home
When? The New Year; January; During a great transformation; Forever
Why? "To sustain longevity, you have to evolve." ~Aries Spears
Yes or No? Maybe after a while; no definitive answer yet

What should I clean?
- Wash windows
- Fix broken faucets or lights
- Work on projects with sustainability

Where are my missing keys?
- You put them down last time you were thinking seriously about something
- They're somewhere, but you won't find them anytime soon

Combos: Ihwaz says *endurance is required for*

Fehu – earning income
Uruz - strength
Thurisaz - defense
Ansuz – speeches
Raido - travel plans
Kaunaz - education
Gebo – a boring party
Wunjo – a windy day
Hagalaz – a crisis
Nauthiz - breaking free
Isa – a slow period
Jera – a difficult year

Pertho - taking risks
Algiz - safety
Sowelo - victory
Tiwaz - peacekeeping
Berkano - parenting
Ehwaz - marriage
Mann- sustainability
Laguz- passing a test
Inguz - gestation
Othala – your legacy
Dagaz - awakening

Perthro

"P"

Luck
Mystery
Fates
Dance

Imagine a set of dice in a cup, ready to be
shaken up and released. Perthro is that
cup, now turned on its side. It is the
moment of the unknown, or the gamble you
took at the craps table. The dice have the
answer, but the Perthro cup itself retains
the mystery.

If you see the cup, remember "Per
throw" to recall the name.

This is a great and powerful Rune,
although not the most helpful. Any answers
you seek are shrouded in mystery.

The reverse of Perthro might be bad
luck, addition, or delusion.

Perthro as:
An action?
- Keep your plan a secret
- Take a gamble
- Go to the casino

A place in your house?
- A dark space
- A less-used room

A place in your city?
- An observatory
- A casino
- A forest trail
- Therapy

A place in the world?
- Monaco
- Las Vegas
- Area 51
- Bermuda Triangle

Something to eat?
- Turducken
- Leftovers
- A melting chocolate ball

A color? Blue, black
A gemstone? Aquamarine

A movie theme? a gamble, a mystery
- Bird Box
- The Lord of the Rings trilogy
- Arrival
- The Game

A new career?
- Casino worker
- Detective
- Night work such as lounge singer, sex worker, or overnight security

Questions answered by Perthro:

Who? The secret keeper; a woman
What? A gamble; a guess; an omen or prophecy
Where? Hidden; downtown at night
When? January; A new moon; The darkest days of winter
Why? "It is only through mystery and madness that the soul is revealed"[16]
Yes or No? Unknown, roll the dice

What should I clean?
- The back of the storage cabinet
- A space you haven't been in awhile

Where are my missing keys?
- Unknown
- Buried and too hidden to see easily
- The poker table

Combos: Perthro says *take a chance on*

Fehu – an expenditure	**Jera** – planting seeds
Uruz – independence	**Algiz** – higher purpose
Thorn – transformation	**Sowelo** – goals
Ansuz-speaking your mind	**Tiwaz** – justice
Raido – a trip	**Berkano** – a fresh start
Kaunaz – education	**Ehwaz** – a partnership
Gebo – a unique gift	**Mannaz** – a good plan
Wunjo – hope	**Laguz** – your dreams
Hagalaz – destruction	**Inguz**– personal growth
Nauthiz – freedom	**Othala** – prosperity
Isa – self-control	**Dagaz** – enlightenment

---

[16] Thomas Moore, *Care of the Soul: A Guide for Cultivating Depth and Sacredness in Everyday Life*

Algiz

"Z"

Protection
Divine Lessons
Elk

Algiz is another Rune that kind of resembles what it is – A great-horned elk or a Valkyrie, standing by to either guard or charge.

Like Thurisaz, this Rune is about protection. Like Ansuz, this Rune is about a divine message. Algiz combines these two forces into one and gives us a message about our higher self, and of being courageous in the face of fear.

If we engage in right action, the Valkyries will defend us.

The reverse of Algiz is fear, or a loss of connection to divine messages.

Algiz as:
An action?
- Follow your instincts
- Check the home security system

A place in your house?
- A prayer or meditation space
- The fence or the walls
- A new project

A place in your city?
- A park
- An old battleground
- The edge of town
- A book store

A place in the world?
- Banff National Park, Alberta
- Rocky Mountain National Park, CO
- Vortexes, AZ
- Allahabad, India

Something to eat?
- Apples
- Flesh of an animal killed in battle
- Breadsticks

A color? Gold, purple, green
A gemstone? Amethyst

A movie theme? Courage
- Thor: Ragnarok
- The Hobbit
- Three Billboards Outside Ebbing, MO

A new career?
- Mercenary, Peacekeeper
- Life coach, therapist
- United Nations work

Questions answered by Algiz:

Who? The empathic one; the one who has returned from battle
What? A self-fulfilling prophecy
Where? An educational institution; the forest
When? January-February; Imbolc; When inspiration hits
Why? "There are moments when, without really knowing it, we are aware of the presence of angels." ~ Paulo Coelho
Yes or No? Yes. **Reversed?** Maybe, but you must overcome your fears

What should I clean?
- The walls and doorhandles

Where are my missing keys?
- In the front hall

Combos: Algiz says *have courage in the face of*

Fehu - overdue bills
Uruz - illness
Thurisaz - danger
Ansuz- misunderstanding
Raido - immobility
Kaunaz - inability
Gebo - greed
Wunjo - worry
Hagalaz - crisis
Nauthiz - drudgery
Isa - stagnation

Jera - regression
Ihwaz - confusion
Perthro - gambles
Sowelo - gullibility
Tiwaz - injustice
Berkano - healing
Ehwaz - betrayal
Mannaz - depression
Laguz - emotions
Inguz - impotence
Othala - poverty
Dagaz - cataclysmic change

Sowelo

"ss"

**Inspiration
Victory
Sun**

Sowelo is another Rune that looks exactly
how it means - it is an S, for Sun,
representing happiness, joy, and success.
It is also a lightning bolt, representing a
flash of inspiration or an instance of
victory and excitement!

Sowelo also cannot be reversed, as the
sun does not hide when it is out, and the
lightning cannot be tamed when inspiration
hits. To find its negative interpretation,
you would have to place it with other
Runes.

Sowelo as:
An action?
- Have an adventure
- Light a campfire
- Celebrate successes

A place in your house?
- A sun-facing window
- The literal sun room

A place in your city?
- A sunny park
- A lamp store
- A view of the sunset

A place in the world?
- Australia
- Lake Maracaibo, Venezuela
- The Land of the Midnight Sun (Far North or South, depending on season)

Something to eat?
- Corn
- Mushrooms
- Sun-dried tomatoes

A color? White, silver, yellow
A gemstone? Ruby

A movie theme? Joy, success, inspiration
- Ferris Bueller's Day Off
- The Theory of Everything
- Moana
- Inside Out

A new career?
- Teacher or tutor
- Amusement park or Cruise Ship operator
- Park ranger or other outdoor job

Questions answered by Sowelo:

Who? A child at play; the happiest person you know
What? The Sun; sudden inspiration
Where? A sunny location
When? The end of February; A sunny day; A lightning storm
Why? "Those who bring sunshine into the lives of others cannot keep it from themselves." – J.M. Barrie
Yes or No? YES!

What should I clean?
- The windows
- Light fixtures

Where are my missing keys?
- In a sunny spot

Combos: Sowelo says *victory and success will be attained through*

Fehu – transactions
Uruz – persistence
Thurisaz – strength
Ansuz - speech
Raido – travel
Kaunaz – education
Gebo – giving
Wunjo – hope
Hagalaz – surrender
Nauthiz – resistance
Isa – self-control

Jera – patience
Ihwaz - perseverance
Perthro – taking risks
Algiz - spirituality
Tyr – self-sacrifice
Berkano - rebirth
Ehwaz - teamwork
Mannaz - intellect
Laguz – psychic power
Inguz – inner growth
Othala - inheritance
Dagaz - daylight

Tyr's Aett

The Norse god Tyr represents justice
and victory. The Runes in this aett,
while more spiritual than practical,
are about life, death, humanity and
enlightenment.

Tiwaz
"t"

Justice
Warrior
The War-God, Tyr

Tyr was the Norse god of treaties and justice. His Rune resembles an arrow, and when upright it points to the North star, both symbols that are representative of his warrior spirit and guiding light.

Plenty of other Runes indicate a warrior mindset, as the Vikings were a war-prone people. However, Tiwaz is less about violence and battle, and more about responsibility, justice, and self-sacrifice.

The reverse of Tiwaz is injustice, defeat, tyranny, or mental paralysis.

Tiwaz as:
An action?
- Sacrifice yourself now for a larger reward later
- Take stairs instead of the elevator

A place in your house?
- The hallway
- A doorway
- The fridge or freezer

A place in your city?
- A court
- An archery school
- A nonprofit organization
- A dog park

A place in the world?
- Eyam, England
- The Hague, Netherlands
- The Caribbean sea

Something to eat?
- Fruit
- Vegetables
- Food that others in the household do not want to eat
- A healthy breakfast

A color? Red
A gemstone? Coral

A movie theme? Sacrifice, Justice
- Prison Break
- Erin Brockovich
- My Cousin Vinny
- Avengers

A new career?
- Psychotherapy
- Historian
- Artist, Writer, Creative
- Caregiver
- Justice

Questions answered by Tiwaz:

Who? A person willing to sacrifice themselves; a parent; a teacher
What? A peacekeeping mission
Where? North; a place where sacrifices are made
When? February-March; during a fight
Why? "Every step toward the goal of justice requires sacrifice, suffering, and struggle; the tireless exertions and passionate concern of dedicated individuals." ~ Martin Luther King, Jr.
Yes or No? Yes **Reversed?** No

Combos: Tiwaz says *sacrifice yourself for*

Fehu – a fresh start
Uruz – survival
Thurisaz – protection
Ansuz - meaning
Raido– the right path
Kaunaz – experience
Gebo - your talents
Wunjo - joy
Hagal– radical change
Nauthiz – innovation
Isa – identity
Jera – progress

Ihwaz - longevity
Perthro – playtime
Algiz – a higher self
Sowelo - victory
Berkano - a fresh start
Ehwaz – the team
Mannaz - humanity
Laguz - imagination
Inguz – self growth
Othala – your homeland
Dagaz - awakening

Berkano
"b"

Birth
Fertility
Nourishment
The Birch Tree

In the far North, the birch tree is the first deciduous tree to bloom in the springtime, and the first growth to colonize after devastation such as fire or logging. Birches grow fast and bring with them new life, both flora and fauna.

Therefore Berkano, meaning "birch goddess" and looking like a B, is the Rune of babies, birth, and becoming.

The reverse of Berkano is insecurity, deceit, or infertility.

Berkano as:
An action?
- Adopt a pet
- Have a baby
- Redecorate
- Build something

A place in your house?
- The dining room
- Kitchen projects
- crafts area
- A fertile garden

A place in your city?
- School
- Supermarket
- Hospital
- Garden nursery

A place in the world?
- Wildfires region
- New Zealand
- Finnmark, Norway
- Canada

Something to eat?
- Lasagna
- Something homemade and filling
- Natural, whole grain foods

A color? Dark green, yellow
A gemstone? Moonstone

A movie theme? Motherhood, rebirth
- Knocked Up
- March of the Penguins
- Jurassic World

A new career?
- Gardener
- Nanny, babysitter, Mom
- Massage therapist
- Secret keeper, such as magician or lawyer

Questions answered by Berkano:

Who? a Mom; a mother figure; a grandmother figure; mother earth
What? A garden
Where? Mom's house; a garden; a rocking chair
When? When the baby is born (literal or metaphoric); End of March; Spring; Easter/Ostara
Why? "If we had no winter, the spring would not be so pleasant; if we did not sometimes taste of adversity, prosperity would not be so welcome." ~Anne Bradstreet
Yes or No? Yes **Reversed?** No

What should I clean?
- The living room
- The nursery

Where are my missing keys?
- Mom has them

Combos: Berkano says *it is up to you to create your own*

Fehu – higher income
Uruz – independence
Thurisaz – safety
Ansuz - communication
Raido – travel
Kaunaz – education
Gebo – gifts
Wunjo - joy
Hagal– radical change
Nauthiz – innovation
Isa – focus
Jera – harvest

Ihwaz - enlightenment
Perthro – destiny
Algiz – spirituality
Sowelo - wholeness
Tyr - justice
Ehwaz – trust in team
Mannaz - memories
Laguz - dreams
Inguz - evolution
Othala - legacy
Dagaz - enlightenment

Ehwaz
"eh"

**Teamwork
Partnership
Horse**

Not to be confused with Ihwaz - which means
yew tree and represents a solitary quest -
Ehwaz means horse and represents teamwork,
emotions, and friendship.

Yes, Ehwaz looks like the letter M,
but it also kind of looks like a horse and
it *means* horse, so that is helpful. Horses
are also partners, so recalling the meaning
is easy once you remember that it is a
horse not an M. However, remembering the
sound is a bit more difficult. It looks
like a letter M but sounds like "eh."

This is another silly trick, but when
you see the M, remember the phrase *"there's
no I in Tea**M**."* There's no I in Ehwaz. Grab
your team, get on your horses, and go!

The reverse of Ehwaz is enemy,
mistrust, or disharmony.

Ehwaz as:
An action?
- Invite a friend to help with a project
- Get married
- Hang out with your pet

A place in your house?
- A project room
- The pet's room
- The garage
- The loveseat

A place in your city?
- An equestrian center
- A petting zoo
- A great date night spot
- A park

A place in the world?
- Paris
- Ireland
- South Africa
- Iceland

Something to eat?
- Bananas
- Something you made with a friend

A color? Grey, white
A gemstone? Calcite

A movie theme? Teamwork, horses
- The Avengers franchise
- Zootopia
- Seabiscuit or Secretariat

A new career?
- Construction
- Horse trainer
- Sports
- Interior designer
- Human Resources

Questions answered by Ehwaz:

Who? A team member; a life partner
What? A relationship
Where? Near animals
When? The beginning of April; The week after a wedding; At a large gathering
Why? "It is the difficult horses that have the most to give you." ~Lendon Gray
Yes or No? Yes **Reversed?** No

What should I clean?
- The kitchen
- The kitty litter
- Complete a project that is bugging you

Where are my missing keys?
- Where you were last with a partner

Combos: Ehwaz says *develop a harmonious relationship with*

Fehu – financial flow
Uruz – physical health
Thurisaz – giants
Ansuz – the divine
Raido– your car
Kaunaz – teachers
Gebo – giving
Wunjo – friends
Hagal– bad weather
Nauthiz – restraint
Isa – yourself
Jera – ups and downs

Ihwaz – mysteries
Perthro – the unknown
Algiz – the divine plan
Sowelo – the sun
Tyr – law and order
Berkano – motherhood
Mannaz – humanity
Laguz – imagination
Inguz – your self
Othala – your homeland
Dagaz – your ideal self

Mannaz

"m"

Humankind
The Mind
Education

Mannaz looks like a funny 'm,' and means humankind. If we imagine that the extra lines on the M are part of a knot, we can recognize the meaning of Mannaz to be interconnectedness, the development of intellect, and the stability we get from being together and learning.

Mannaz is also associated with thinking, planning, and mortality. It is the quintessential Rune of the human condition.

The reverse of Mannaz is collective ignorance, elitism, depression, or other mental illness.

Mannaz as:
An action?
- Think
- Advocate for social programs

A place in your house?
- The mailbox
- The bathroom (the thinker on the throne!)

A place in your city?
- Hospice care
- A startup incubator
- A University

A place in the world?
- Humanity itself
- San Francisco
- Toronto
- Shanghai

Something to eat?
- A casserole
- Soup
- Rice, grains
- Pizza

A color? Deep red, green
A gemstone? Garnet

A movie theme? The human condition
- The Pursuit of Happyness
- The Shawshank Redemption
- Being John Malkovich
- Coco

A new career?
- I/O Psychologist
- Forensics
- Grief counselor
- Urban Planning

Questions answered by Mannaz:

Who? A prophet or teacher
What? An opportunity to learn
Where? A school
When? The end of April; adulthood; graduation
Why? "We are very, very small, but we are profoundly capable of very, very big things." ~Stephen Hawking
Yes or No? Yes. **Reversed?** There are flaws.

What should I clean?
- The living room or social area
- Your mind (meditate)
- The bookshelf

Where are my missing keys?
- Under the couch
- On the dining room table

Combos: Mannaz says *work with others to establish a*

Fehu – startup biz
Uruz – workout plan
Thurisaz - defense
Ansuz - conversation
Raido– travel plan
Kaunaz – technique
Gebo – exchange
Wunjo - fellowship
Hagal– crisis plan
Nyd – chores schedule
Isa – quiet
Jera – farm

Ihwaz – business plan
Perthro – game night
Algiz – religion
Sowelo – action plan
Tyr – fair judgement
Berkano - sanctuary
Ehwaz – great team
Lagz– collective memory
Inguz – growth plan
Othala - legacy
Dagaz – paradigm shift

Laguz
"l"

Subconscious
Imagination
Emotions
Lake

Laguz means lake and sounds like "L" which is easy enough. It almost looks like an L too, if that L was reflected in a mirror on the ceiling.

Like a mysterious reflection, Laguz covers the subconscious, dreams, emotions, and psychic ability - things that are just out of reach from our logical mind.

Mannaz was the conscious intellect. Laguz is the subconscious shadow.

The reverse of Laguz is emotional manipulation, fantastical ideas, fear, or avoidance.

Laguz as:
An action?
- Meditate
- Drink water
- Practice the occult
- Take a nap and record your dreams

A place in your house?
- A pagan altar
- The sink or tub
- The bedroom

A place in your city?
- A psychic
- A children's museum
- A therapist's office
- A yoga studio

A place in the world?
- Tibet
- Fatima or Lourdes
- Delphi
- Kenya
- Macedonia

Something to eat?
- Water
- Nuts and seeds
- Herbal tea
- Raw chocolate

A color? Turquoise, green
A gemstone? Pearl

A movie theme? Intuitive wisdom, water
- Star Wars
- Hidden Figures
- The Shape of Water

A new career?
- Marine research or biology
- Psychic or intuitive healer
- Psychologist
- Environmental Scientist

Questions answered by Laguz:

Who? Your subconscious; an intuitive person
What? A mystery hidden under the surface
Where? In your own head; at the lake
When? The beginning of May; at night; in your dreams
Why? "Who looks outside, dreams; who looks inside, awakes." ~Carl Jung
Yes or No? Maybe; your unconscious knows.

What should I clean?
- The tub or shower
- The blinds

Where are my missing keys?
- In water
- Somewhere you were in a moment of Zen or Highway hypnosis[17]

Combos: *Laguz says you are ignoring subconscious messages about your*

Fehu – money	**Ihwaz** - mortality
Uruz – independence	**Perthro** – destiny
Thurisaz – strength	**Algiz** – higher self
Ansuz - communication	**Sigel** – life purpose
Raido– vehicle	**Tyr** - principles
Kaunaz – craft	**Berkano** - fertility
Gebo – talents	**Ehwaz** - team
Wunjo - happiness	**Mannaz** - memory
Hagal– crises	**Inguz** – inner child
Nyd – life lessons	**Othala** - estate
Isa - identity	**Dagaz** – ideal self
Jera – progress	

---

[17] Highway hypnosis is unconscious awareness, when attentions are occupied with things other than the task at hand.

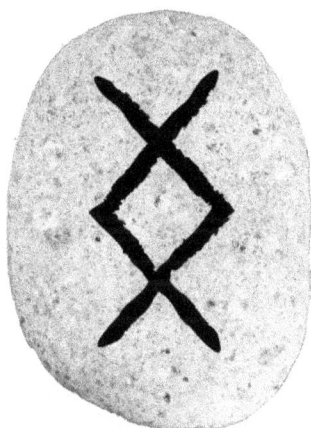

Inguz
"ng"

Creation
Internal growth
Hero
Seed

Inguz is created two ways – either a diamond shape, or something that looks like a DNA strand. I prefer the DNA strand, because it is a reminder that Inguz is about internal growth. It literally means "seed" and is about the creation and power of the self.

The seed has been planted by the divine, and it is up to you to nurture it.

Inguz cannot be reversed, as evolution happens whether we control it or not. Negative interpretations would depend upon other Runes in the reading.

Inguz as:
An action?
- Create a ritual of self-care
- Meditate on your life goals

A place in your house?
- A soft carpet
- A home gym
- An art piece that is special to you

A place in your city?
- A quiet room at the office
- The changing room at the gym
- A flower display or festival

A place in the world?
- Bali
- Iceland
- The Appalachian or Pacific coast trail

Something to eat?
- Fatty fish
- Muesli and Granola bars
- Spring water

A color? Yellow, orange
A gemstone? Amber

A movie theme? Evolving yourself
- Wild
- Eat, Pray, Love
- Forrest Gump

A new career?
- Manual labor or agriculture
- Self-employment
- Careers using tools and creative expression

Questions answered by Inguz:

Who? Someone starting over; a baby
What? DNA; an idea you had last winter
Where? A freshly planted garden
When? The end of May; Spring; today
Why? "You can, you should, and if you're brave enough to start, you will." ~Stephen King
Yes or No? Yes, but ruminate a bit more

What should I clean?
- Your laundry
- Your desk
- Your creative space

Where are my missing keys?
- Where you started the last project

Combos: Inguz says *you possess the inner power to grow and develop*

Fehu – more money
Uruz – strength
Thurisaz - enthusiasm
Ansuz– communication
Raido– travel plans
Kaunaz – art
Gebo – innate gifts
Wunjo – happiness
Hagal– self-analysis
Nauthiz – effort
Isa – focus
Jera – good harvest

Ihwaz– enlightenment
Perthro – your luck
Algiz – a higher self
Sowelo - mastery
Tiwaz - principles
Berkano – new life
Ehwaz – a team
Mannaz– social order
Laguz– psychic power
Othala – a legacy
Dagaz – spiritual awakening

Othala

"oh"

Legacy
Inheritance
Homeland

Where Fehu was wealth that is fluid, Othala is wealth that is generational. Fehu is new money, Odal is old money, and thus they are found at nearly opposite ends of the Runes[18].

Othala might also represent an inherited talent or behavioral characteristic, such as a legacy of fine chefs in a family. I like to imagine Othala as a fish being passed down from a parent to a child, and the child saying "*oh*, this is my legacy."

Reversed, Othala might represent the cycles of poverty or negative behavioral traits that families pass down.

---

[18] Some Rune interpreters put Othala at the end, but as Othala represents preparing final affairs, and Dagal is a solstice and enlightenment, Othala here is the penultimate.

Othala as:
An action?
- Write your will
- Look to your ancestors for wisdom

A place in your house?
- Photos of your family
- The important documents
- The walls

A place in your city?
- A senior center
- Your lawyer's office
- a market
- a place of wealth, legacy

A place in the world?
- Monaco
- Japan
- Hong Kong
- Iceland
- San Marino

Something to eat?
- An heirloom recipe
- Baked goods

A color? Dark yellow
A gemstone? Ruby

A movie theme? Legacy, inheritance
- Mr. Deeds
- Anastasia
- Batman

A new career?
- Property developer or house flipper
- Antiques dealer
- Join the family business
- Retire

Questions answered by Othala:

Who? A matriarch or patriarch
What? A legacy
Where? On the family property
When? The beginning of June; when affairs are in order; at the reading of a will
Why? "Someone is sitting in the shade today because someone planted a tree a long time ago." ~Warren Buffett
Yes or No? Yes **Reversed?** No, and be careful of wrong traits being passed down.

What should I clean?
- The house you'll eventually pass down
- Your heirlooms

Where are my missing keys?
- Either your parents have them, or you handed them to a child

Combos: Othala says *prepare now to leave a legacy of*

Fehu – liquid wealth
Uruz – survival
Thurisaz - protection
Ansuz – reason
Raido – travel
Ken – artistic skill
Gebo – generosity
Wunjo – fellowship
Hagal– opportunity
Nauthiz – hard work
Isa – self-control
Jera – good harvest

Ihwaz - immortality
Perthro – good luck
Algiz – education
Sowelo - confidence
Tiwaz – law & order
Berkano - healing
Ehwaz - partnership
Mannaz - memories
Laguz - imagination
Inguz – self growth
Dagaz - enlightenment

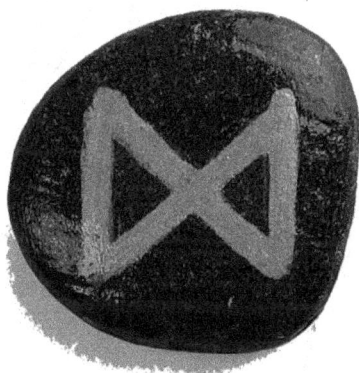

Dagaz
"d"

Enlightenment
Awakening
Day

The final Rune of the Elder Futhark
alphabet is not so final at all. Dagaz
represents enlightenment, daytime, and the
unity of heaven and Earth. Resembling an
infinity symbol, Dagaz reminds us that
endings are just new beginnings, and that
life and fulfillment will circle back at
any time.

Dagaz has no reverse, as nothing in
this existence ever truly ends. However,
placed with more ominous Runes it could
mean an inability to visualize the future,
or cataclysmic and devastating change.

Dagaz as:
An action?
- Change jobs
- Have a baby
- Obtain enlightenment

A place in your house?
- The house in its entirety
- Your storage unit

A place in your city?
- The museum
- A high viewpoint
- A theme park
- A fortune teller

A place in the world?
- Machu Picchu
- Tibet
- Jerusalem
- Scandinavia
- A place representing the start of a new chapter (of yourself, humanity, etc)

Something to eat?
- Coffee
- Raw fruits and veggies
- Water
- Tea

A color? No color or all colors
A gemstone? Any. Also peridot

A movie theme? Completion, enlightenment
- Groundhog Day
- Wall-E
- Legally Blonde
- Cloud Atlas

A new career?
- Natural resources or land use
- Data scientist
- Writer, speaker, teacher
- Your life's purpose

Questions answered by Dagaz:

Who? The person going through a significant life change
What? Enlightenment
Where? A place of spiritual awakening
When? The summer Solstice; The end of June; Daytime; During a significant life change
Why? "This is my simple religion. There is no need for temples; no need for complicated philosophy. Our own brain, our own heart is our temple; the philosophy is kindness." - Dalai Lama
Yes or No? Yes!

What should I clean?

- Everything - book a day off and do the whole house

Where are my missing keys?

- In a place that means everything to you, such as your baby's crib

Combos: Dagaz says *you are transforming into*

Fehu - a new role
Uruz - a survivor
Thurisaz - a hero
Ansuz - a teacher
Raido - a traveler
Kaunaz - a thinker
Gebo - a giver
Wunjo - an optimist
Hagalaz - crisis
Nyd - a hard worker
Isa - self-control
Jera - harmony with the land

Ihwaz - immortality
Peorth- the luckiest
Algiz - a higher self
Sowelo - wholeness
Tyr - a spiritual warrior
Berkano - a nurturer
Ehwaz - a partner
Mannaz - an analytic
Laguz - a psychic
Inguz - an earth god
Othala - your enlightened self

The Blank Rune

Many commercial sets of Runes come with a
blank stone. This is not a traditional
stone the Germanic tribes used when
Runecasting, but it is not wrong to include
it if you want more answers.

A typical interpretation of this blank
stone is that it foretells of a fated
event, and that the situation, good or bad,
is out of the questioner's control.

Other Runes might explain what the
forthcoming uncontrollable situation might
involve.

Acknowledgements

I use Runes every day to boss me around, tell me where things are, and convince me to work on new projects. However, Runes are merely stones, and stones cannot inspire, nor can they assist. This book would not exist without the inspiration and assistance of a few key people.

My mother, Margaret, who bought the very first copy of *Applied Tarot*, read it the night it was delivered, then emailed me a list of all the copy errors I had made. I sent *Applied Runes* to her in advance of publication this time. Thanks Mum.

Tammy, Mindi, Rhiannon, Allan, and all my writer friends who not only forked over money for the first book (when they could have asked me for a free one!) but who cheered me on for this second book, too. Although we met writing fiction, their support of my nonfiction work is unending.

My cat, Leopold, who chewed my Runes, slept on my keyboard, clawed my face, and tried many other ways to stop me from writing. Daily battles with him were both a burden and an inspiration. Leopold embodies the violent nature of Thurisaz, and if I can fight him and win, I can do anything.

Lastly, my three kids, wonderful husband, and everyone who subjected themselves to random Rune spreads along the way.

Image Credits

About the Author

Emily Paper grew up in Ontario, Canada and
spent much of her time in solitude seeking
mystical inspiration. Credit for her Hermit-
like intuitive development goes to her parents,
who often sent the kids deep into the woods
assuming they could survive on their own. They
almost all did!

After completing an undergraduate degree
in Psychology from the University of Waterloo
and advanced studies in technical writing,
Emily settled into a stable job in technical
support. Everything was fine, then suddenly a
pandemic!

During the shutdown, Emily returned to
her childhood passion for claircognizance and
solitude, obtained certification in Feng Shui,
and started Tarot and runic consulting.

Today, Emily is a divination and Feng
Shui specialist, but with over 35 years of
random fortune telling experience, it took
losing a set of car keys to inspire her to
write about it. Her first book, *Applied Tarot*,
might help you find your keys, too.

Emily lives in Washington State with her
husband, and any money they earn goes straight
to the college bursar's office for their three
studious children.

Emily can be found wandering around social
media, and at www.emilypaper.com

Applied Tarot
REVERSED

**An Excessively Practical Guide to
Interpreting Reversed Tarot Cards**

What movie should you watch when you pull

The Hermit reversed?

You should still watch **The Truman Show!**

I will never stop recommending the Truman Show. But when you watch it this time, pay attention to the extra cinematic and storyline details you may have missed before - the travel agent who arrives with a makeup bib on. The friend/actor who "got pneumonia" probably as an excuse for a work vacation.
The Truman Show is fascinating.

Follow emilypaper.com for more information

Notes

www.ingramcontent.com/pod-product-compliance
Lightning Source LLC
Chambersburg PA
CBHW070851280326
41934CB00008B/1394